Carving Flat-Plane Style
CARICATURES

Step-by-Step Instructions & Patterns for 50 Projects

Carving Flat-Plane Style
CARICATURES

Step-by-Step Instructions & Patterns for 50 Projects

by Harley Refsal

A *Woodcarving Illustrated* Book
www.WoodcarvingIllustrated.com

FOX CHAPEL
PUBLISHING

Acknowledgments

The Swedish Institute (Stockholm), Döderhultarn Museum (Oskarshamn), Norwegian Foreign Ministry (Oslo and New York), Norwegian Folk Museum (Oslo), Viking Ship Museum (Oslo), Nordmanns-Forbundet (Oslo), Norway-America Association (Oslo), Maihaugen (Lillehammer), Akademiet (Rauland), E.L.C.A.-Faculty Research Grant (Chicago), Sons of Norway (Minneapolis), American-Swedish Institute (Minneapolis), Vesterheim (Decorah), and Luther College (Decorah) have all provided me with financial and/or moral support in connection with my research. To them as well as to my family, friends, and countless other museum staffers, librarians, and woodcarvers, I extend my sincere appreciation.

Except in the step-by-step demonstrations and as noted otherwise, all of the photographs were taken by Chip Peterson (or me), and many of my carvings were painted by my wife, Norma Refsal.

Carving Flat-Plane Style Caricatures is a revised and updated version of *Art & Technique of Scandinavian Style Woodcarving* (978-1-56523-230-3, 2004). This new edition includes four new patterns; expanded carving and painting instructions; and two new step-by-step projects. Portions of this book were originally published in *Woodcarving Illustrated* magazine. The patterns contained herein are copyrighted by the author. Readers may make copies of these patterns for personal use. The patterns themselves, however, are not to be duplicated for resale or distribution under any circumstances. Any such copying is a violation of copyright law.

ISBN 978-1-56523-858-9

Library of Congress Cataloging-in-Publication Data

Refsal, Harley.
  Carving flat-plane style caricatures / Harley Refsal.
    pages cm
  Includes index.
  ISBN 978-1-56523-858-9
  1. Wood-carving--Norway. 2. Wood-carving--Sweden. 3. Wood-carved figurines--Norway. 4. Wood-carved figurines--Sweden. I. Title.
  TT199.7.R43964 2015
  736'.409481--dc23
                2014047795

To learn more about the other great books from Fox Chapel Publishing,
or to find a retailer near you, call toll-free
800-457-9112 or visit us at *www.FoxChapelPublishing.com*.

Note to Authors: We are always looking for talented authors to write new books. Please send a brief letter describing your idea to Acquisition Editor, 1970 Broad Street, East Petersburg, PA 17520.

Printed in China
First printing

About the Author

Harley Refsal is an internationally recognized figure carver who specializes in Scandinavian-style flat-plane carving. In 1996, he received the St. Olav's Medal from the King of Norway in recognition of his contributions to Norwegian folk art. In 2012, Harley was named the Woodcarver of the Year by *Woodcarving Illustrated* magazine for both reviving the art of flat-plane carving and teaching it across the United States and around the world.

Now the Professor Emeritus of Scandinavian Folk Art at Luther College in Decorah, Iowa, Harley was born and raised on the farm near Hoffman, Minnesota, that was homesteaded by his Norwegian-immigrant grandparents. He began working in wood as a young boy. His father, who was a carpenter and farmer, and a woodworker uncle who lived nearby kept Harley well supplied with wood, tools, and encouragement.

Primarily self-taught, Harley began winning awards in regional and national carving exhibitions in the late 1970s. He also began researching the history of Scandinavian flat-plane carving, with which he had become especially enamored. But soon he discovered that most of the artists who had worked in this style during the height of its popularity in the early decades of the 20th century in both Scandinavia and America had died, and the tradition of flat-plane carving had faded to near-extinction.

Since the 1980s, Harley, who speaks fluent Norwegian, has shared his knowledge of, and skills in, Scandinavian flat-plane carving with thousands of carvers in classes and presentations in North America and Scandinavia. In addition to writing several books on the subject, he has authored many book chapters and magazine articles, and has been featured on numerous radio and television programs, including the PBS Peabody Award-winning series "Craft in America." His name is so integrally linked with the revival of this carving style that it is often referred to as the "Refsal style."

Contents

Getting Started

In this book, the discussion of Scandinavian-style figure carving, and "flat-plane" carving in particular, will deal with a style of carving that developed and became popular in Norway and Sweden. Although Denmark, Finland, and Iceland also comprise part of Scandinavia, I am limiting the discussion to Norway and Sweden, since their conditions and traditions are fairly similar—especially when it comes to figure carving. Therefore, in the context of this book, the term "Scandinavian" will refer primarily to Norway and Sweden. The style of figure carving I will be discussing was common in both countries, but it was far less common in Denmark and Finland and nearly nonexistent in Iceland.

The term "flat-plane carving" stems from a particular style of figure carving—one in which large, flat planes, created by using primarily a knife and perhaps just a gouge or two, were left intact. Smooth, rounded sculpting and sanding were typically not employed in the final finish.

I was introduced to Scandinavian figure carving during my first visit to Norway in 1965. Two years later, while studying at the University of Oslo, I was able to travel more widely throughout Norway as well as in Sweden. Since I had worked with wood and had also done some whittling as a boy, I became interested in the woodcarving traditions of both countries. I was especially intrigued by the small wooden figures I saw in shops and museums.

Upon returning to the United States in 1968, I began to carve figures of my own, using a pocketknife and a wood chisel that my father, a carpenter and farmer, had made from a worn-out file. Since I was unable to locate any carvers creating the style of figures I had seen in Scandinavia, I simply gleaned what information and inspiration I could from photos, articles, and sketches I had made.

One of the articles I eventually ran across featured photos of some carvings by Axel Petersson Döderhultarn, whose rough-hewn figures have made a lasting impression on me. Using only a few well-placed cuts and leaving large, flat planes, he was able to convey fascinating stories in wood.

I had been attempting to tell stories through my figures too, and Döderhultarn's style of carving provided just the means of expression I had been seeking. I began using this style of carving to create objects and figures with which I was familiar, and I began trying to say more by saying less.

After having taught courses throughout North America and Scandinavia, I can't decide which I enjoy more: carving figures myself, or trying to help others develop their skills so that they can tell their own stories in wood. But I can say with certainty that my admiration for the small wooden figures that whispered into my ear half a century ago only keeps on growing.

–HARLEY REFSAL

About Flat-Plane Carving

Dancers, by Axel Petersson Döderhultarn (Döderhultarmuseet, Oskarshamn). Photo: Sven Nilsson.

A Scandinavian carver once remarked, "You can describe traditional handcraft here in our part of the world in three words: wood, wood, wood." While it may be a slight exaggeration, there is a lot of truth in the statement. Until the early 20th century, a high percentage of Nordic folks experienced life in the slow lane. Living on a very small farm, in a log house, they slept in a wooden bed, walked on a wooden (or earthen) floor wearing hand-carved wooden shoes. Breakfast was likely eaten with a wooden spoon from a wooden bowl, after which daily work was done using handmade wooden tools, utensils, machinery, spinning wheels, and looms. And even though those wooden objects were utilitarian, most were embellished with relief or chip carving, or with painted decor.

Some of the carving required a gouge or spoon knife, but the majority of the work described above was done with one single tool: a sturdy, all-purpose fixed-blade—or whittling—knife, worn in a leather sheath at the belt. Knives were handmade by local blacksmiths, but by the end of the 1800s, larger scale production began to appear, making knives affordable to virtually everyone.

Whittling was common in logging camps, where large groups of men gathered each year after the Christmas holiday. The period from January to March was logging season, when ample snow cover made it easier to skid logs out of the forest. Those months afforded men the opportunity to whittle easily portable items during their evening hours in the bunkhouse. A toy for the children back home? How about a carved horse? And a few prolific whittlers undoubtedly created

horses, roosters, and other toys as sale items—a welcome source of additional income.

Did those non-professional woodcarvers, most of whom carved mainly for pleasure or gift-giving rather than for profit, purposely strive to achieve a "flat-plane" look? Probably not, but lacking an arsenal of various gouges and abrasives—available only to a small number of professional, guild-member carvers—the surface of their carvings featured randomly sized flat facets, or planes.

But the resulting whittled, or minimalist, look inspired others, including the early twentieth century Swedish carver Axel Petersson Döderhultarn, mentioned earlier. He felt that those flat planes helped to create the unpolished, chiseled look that brought his characters to life. The hardy rural folk he depicted were not worn smooth by years of rubbing shoulders with other people. By using only a whittling knife, and occasionally a large gouge or two, he was able to let the rugged individualism of his characters remain intact.

Twenty-first century carvers have the same option—to try to say more by saying less. Think flat planes, rather than smoothly rounded countours, as you shape a figure—especially the clothing. Don't overload the figure with unnecessary detail, but let the eye and mind of the viewer fill in the details. It may seem challenging at first to refrain from carving every little detail, but the "difficult art of simplication"—whittling, flat-plane style—becomes more natural and grows more enjoyable and satisfying with each caricature you carve.

Happy flat-plane carving!

Basic Carving Instructions

For two centuries, the government of Norway, trying to protect its artisan guilds, forbade the common people from owning and using any tools other than an axe and a knife. Although we assume some people used illegal tools, the majority simply became very skilled with the two available to them.

Flat-plane carving developed from that tradition, so all of the projects in this book can be carved with just a sharp knife. In addition, I occasionally use a gouge or V-tool for details, and I cut the pattern outlines with a band saw or scroll saw to save some hand carving.

It is important to keep your knife sharp; a sharp knife is actually much safer to work with than a dull one. Keep your knife sharp by using a strop. I strop at least once an hour using aluminum-oxide powder on leather. Also, I highly recommend wearing a Kevlar carving glove while you work.

I use basswood for my carvings because it is easy to carve and paint, and will hold detail. If you want to use a different wood, I suggest pine. Poplar is a little too stringy and, because of its dominant grain, butternut does not work well for painted pieces. Most of the projects presented here were carved with the wood grain running up and down.

Even if you don't plan to carve the projects, read through the instructions for the *Troll King* (page 12) and *Java John* (page 22). The same general instructions apply to most of the projects in the book.

To start any carving, size the pattern as desired and transfer it to the blank. (Measure the pattern to determine the proper size for the blank.) Cut around the outline using a band saw or scroll saw. Then, refer to the pattern to sketch the major body parts (head, torso, arms, legs) onto the blank.

Carve the general shape of the entire figure before adding any details. If you develop one section prematurely and carve all of its details before blocking in the rest of the figure, you may find you have one or more elements in the wrong place in relation to the rest of the carving. Then, you have to carve that section away and start over, or live with a poorly carved figure.

Finally, remember to take your time. Hasty work can result in a mistake on your carving or an accident with one of your tools.

CARVING TIPS

- Rough out the anatomy first to maintain the carving's balance and proportion. Carve the details later.

- Refer to the pattern regularly because you may need to redraw reference lines several times. Keep the big picture in mind. Details are meant to be done last.

- As an advanced carver, I remove large chips. If you are a beginning carver, it is fine to make small cuts at first. Control is more important than removing large chunks of wood.

- It is okay to fix your mistakes. Some accidents can lead you in a direction that is much more interesting than your original idea.

- Remember to stop and strop frequently. You should strop at least once an hour. I use aluminum-oxide powder on leather.

- Carve in good light. If carving outdoors, in natural light, the best light seems to be what I call open shade. Avoid direct sunlight and intense shade.

Painting and Finishing

As much as I enjoy carving a piece, I also enjoy painting it. It's always surprising how long a good paint job takes. Don't rush the process—the painting time can almost rival the time needed to carve.

I use basswood for most of my projects. Light in color and lacking a strong figured grain, basswood is easy to carve and ideal for painting. I prefer to use acrylics diluted with water to create a wash, because I want the wood grain to show through the paint.

I paint with a chisel or angle brush because it allows me to reach the corners and edges of the carving. A liner brush is helpful to paint very small areas, get into the tiniest of corners, and for fine detail work, such as painting eyebrows.

Mixing a Wash

To mix paint washes, pour a small amount of water— only a few teaspoonfuls—into a container, and then add a few drops of paint. Most of the paint containers I use have a top that can dispense individual drops. You can use an eyedropper if desired. Stir the paint and water together, and then test the mixture by painting on newspaper. The newsprint should be easily visible through the color wash. If the mixture is too thin, continue to add paint, drop by drop, and keep testing until you achieve the desired result.

Painting a Carving

Check that you have a clean cut between areas of different colors. I keep a knife handy to correct cuts between the colors if needed.

Start painting on the back of the carving or in some other less noticeable area. Beginning to paint in an inconspicuous place enables you to get used to the feel of the brush and paint on wood. This approach helps you become more comfortable with painting before moving on to a more difficult or more noticeable area.

Create a strategy before you begin. Acrylics dry quickly, so start with a color that can dry while you paint the next part. Avoid painting next to a still-wet color. If you would rather not wait for paint to air dry, use a hair dryer to speed up the process.

Finishing a Carving

After the paint is thoroughly dry, brush on Johnson Paste Wax, following the instructions on the can. Brush it on vigorously using an old toothbrush, and then wipe off the excess wax with paper towels. Use a toothpick to remove any embedded wax bits to avoid them hardening in deep, hard-to-clean areas. Then, buff or wipe the carving with a soft cloth.

PAINTING TIPS

- When you are done carving, check that you have carved away all of the raw wood. Uncarved wood accepts paint and finish differently than carved wood and will be visible on the finished project.

- If you notice pencil or oil marks on the completed carving, wash it with soap and water, rinse it thoroughly, and let it dry before you paint it.

- Paint light colors before painting adjacent dark colors. Dark paint will layer over light paint, but not vice-versa. Let each color dry before painting the adjacent areas.

- I make color washes by mixing about 10 drops of water to 1 drop of paint. For darker washes, use 5 to 7 drops of water per 1 drop of paint. Use full-strength black and white paint for the eyes.

- I like to imagine that my carvings represent new immigrants, farm folk, and outdoorsy people, so I generally use muted shades of brown, gray, blue, green, and red for their clothing. You are welcome to use your favorite colors and combinations, of course.

Troll King

Trolls are popular subjects in Scandinavian folklore. While some trolls are depicted as ugly and mean, others are said to have lived near humans long enough to be merely gruff. If you prefer, you can think of this character as a grumpy old man instead of a troll.

Troll King: Defining Basic Shapes

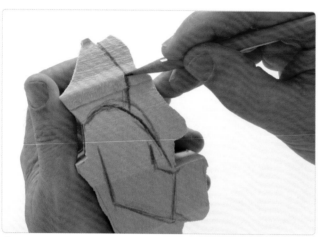

1 Sketch the pattern lines. Transfer the pattern to the blank and cut the outline with a scroll saw or band saw. Then, draw the main pattern lines on the front, right, left, and bottom of the carving blank.

2 Rough out the major shapes. Begin to shape the legs and stomach. Remove wood from both sides of the troll's face and above the shoulders, making sure the face stands out from the rest of the body.

3 Redraw the pattern lines. Move down to the chest and restore any anatomy lines that were carved away. Lines for the arms and the waist become important points of reference. Remove wood in front of the arms to give them definition.

4 Define the arms. Once you have finished removing the wood from the front of the arms, draw the lines for the arms on the back of the blank. Remove wood up to those lines so the arms are separated from the body.

Troll King: Refining the Body

5 Shape the feet. Remove wood from behind the heels. Then, rough out the inside of the feet, making a parentheses shape ( ) for this area. Rough out the front of the feet. Bare feet give the troll an earthy look. Leave the bottom of the feet flat so the finished troll will stand steadily.

6 Shape the troll's back. Start to shape the back of the hair, arms, legs, and body. Think of this step as removing the corners from these areas. Shape the top of the head.

Delve into flat-plane carving with this beginner project from a master carver.

Troll King: Refining the Body

7 Shape the arms. As you carve each arm, aim for a shape that has three planes instead of a smooth cylinder.

8 Mark the legs. Before shaping the legs, mark the height of the crotch where the seat of the pants meets the legs. Make the same mark on the front of the carving. Then, shape the legs.

9 Shape the feet. Once you have finished shaping the legs, carve the cuffs at the bottom of the trousers and the feet.

10 Define the trousers. Carve away saw marks from the troll's back and define the top of his trousers.

Troll King: Carving the Face

11 Separate the nose. Redraw any reference lines that were carved away. Begin shaping the face by making stop cuts beside the nose and removing the waste wood from the cheeks. Remember this style of carving emphasizes flat planes rather than rounded surfaces.

12 Add an expression. After the initial shaping of the face, draw the smile (or frown) lines. Remove wedges of wood along the lines to separate the cheeks from the mouth area.

13 Carve the mouth and chin. Draw and carve the mouth. Next, shape the chin. Keep thinking in terms of flat planes instead of rounded surfaces.

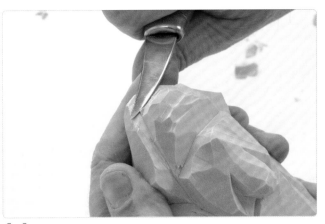

14 Shape the nose and forehead. Shape the nose. Then, make two large V-cuts above the nose to create a flat surface for the eyes. Shape the forehead, and then carve away any saw marks on his hair.

Troll King: Adding Details

15 Sketch the stick location. Draw a line on the front and side of the hand to represent the walking stick being grasped by the extended hand. These are guidelines for drilling a hole for the stick.

16 Drill the hole for the stick. Drill the hole first, and then shape the hand around the hole. Drill a ¼" (6mm)-diameter hole for the stick, making sure to sight along the guidelines drawn in the previous step.

17 Carve the hand around the hole. The hand consists of three basic planes—the back of the hand, the base of the fingers up to the first knuckle, and the tips of the fingers. Align the plane for the base of the fingers with the forearm. Carve the planes, and then rough shape the thumb as it fits around the hole for the stick.

DRILLING A CARVING TIPS

- When a project calls for drilling a hole in a hand, it's a good idea to shape the hand around the hole. Drill the hole first and then carve around it.

- Work up to the final size of the hole by using increasingly larger bits—for example, ⅛" (3mm) to 3/16" (5mm) to ¼" (6mm).

- Use 6" (152mm)-long bits, so you can drill close to the carving without the drill getting in the way.

Troll King: Adding Details

18 **Finish shaping the hand.** Separate the fingers using V-cuts. As you finish the thumb, be sure it curves upward. This curve distinguishes it from the other fingers.

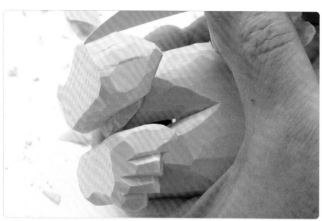

19 **Carve the toes.** Sketch a big toe and three other toes for each foot. Start by defining the big toe. Be sure the big toe curves upward, similar to the way the thumb curves on the hand. Shape the other toes and round the sides and arches of the feet.

20 **Carve the clothing.** Finish carving the trousers. Then, carve wrinkles or creases at the back of the knees and inside of the elbows. Roll the knife into the wood to achieve these folds.

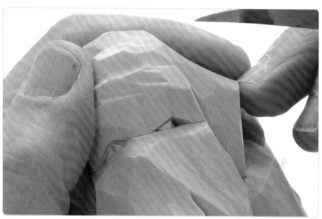

21 **Carve the eyes and hair.** Draw a triangle for each eye. Score the entire triangle with the point of a knife. Remove half of the triangle so the troll is looking to the left. Texture the hair by carving with small rolling slices.

Troll King: Painting the Figure

22 **Thin the paint.** Mix Hooker's green and water. Test the mixture by painting on newspaper. Adjust the mixture if necessary until you can read the newsprint through the color. If you want to make the color a little more woodsy, add a drop or two of brown iron oxide to the green.

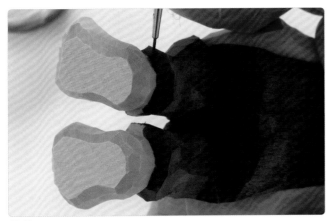

23 **Paint the trousers.** Start painting on the back of the trousers and then paint the front. Don't worry about painting with the grain or facets. Once you have finished painting the majority of the trousers, use the liner brush to get any hard-to-reach areas, such as the cuffs.

24 **Paint the hair.** Create gray by combining ten parts antique white, one part black, and water. Paint the hair. Add a dot of antique white to the gray and use the edge of the brush to highlight the hair.

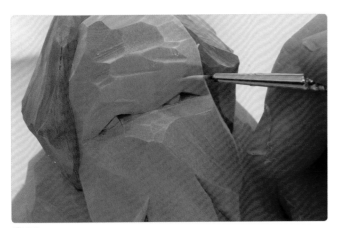

25 **Add the eyebrows.** Give the troll eyebrows using a liner brush and the same color used for the hair highlights.

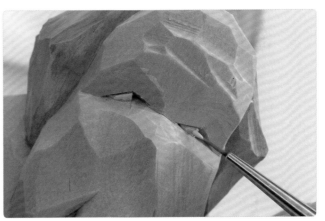

26 **Paint the eyes.** Rinse the liner brush with water before using it to apply full-strength antique white to the eyeballs.

27 **Paint the shirt.** Combine twenty parts water with one part tomato spice. Add a little bit of brown iron oxide if desired. Begin painting the shirt on the back. Use the liner brush for hard-to-reach areas, such as around the face.

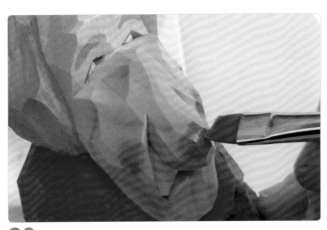

28 **Redden the face.** Brush water on the areas you want to tint. Then, dry the brush thoroughly by wiping it on a paper towel. With the dry brush, place small dots of tomato spice on the the cheeks, the nose, and the forehead.

ори. ..

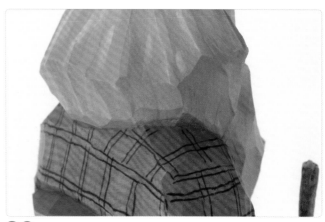

30 Draw the plaid lines. Look at a real flannel shirt for reference. Use a fine-point marker to draw the lines of the troll's shirt. Make the lines follow the bends of the arms. A double line minimizes any unevenness in the fabric or shakiness in your hands.

29 Blend the blush. Smooth the red to blend it with the surrounding areas. Use a damp brush if needed to blend the red thoroughly with the surrounding areas.

PAINT FIX-UPS

If paint ends up where it doesn't belong, simply carve it off.

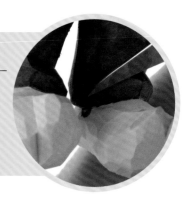

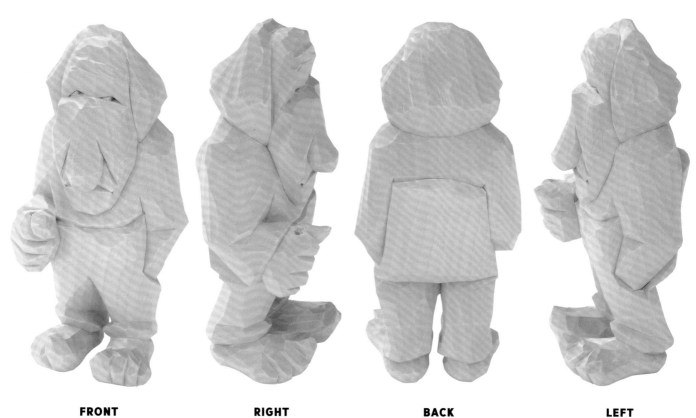

FRONT   **RIGHT**   **BACK**   **LEFT**

Troll King Patterns

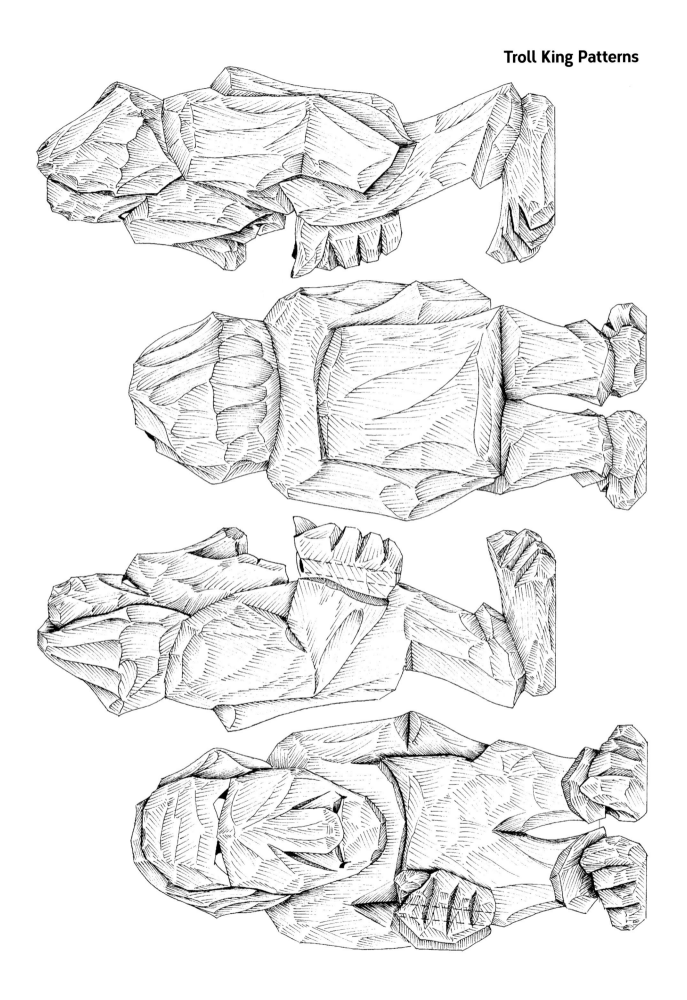

Troll Queen

Even a troll king must have a queen. To make this one, refer to the instructions for the previous project, adapting them as necessary. For instance, smooth the feet and give them a slight point rather than carving toes. Round the exposed right hand and carve fingers, similar to those on the left hand. Make the face slightly rounder and fuller. Pattern the dress as you choose; I dipped the end of a paintbrush to make dotted flowers. Refer to the photo to carve a topper for the staff, or see pages 29, 35, and 37 for alternate accessories.

RIGHT

FRONT

LEFT

BACK

Thanks to her simple dress and kerchief, the *Troll Queen* is easy to carve.

Troll Queen Patterns

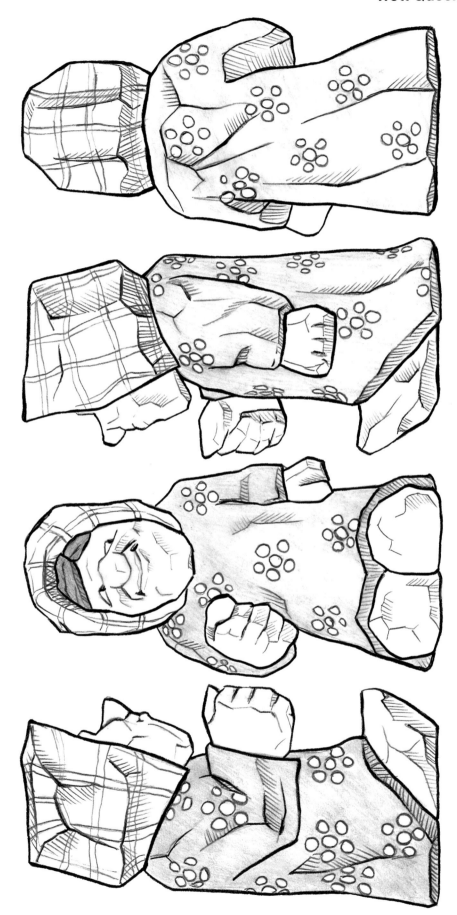

Java John

"Java John" Peterson used to work in a lumberyard, where he picked up his addictions to two specific aromas: coffee and freshly cut wood. He prefers to carve with just a single knife because it's quiet, affordable, and portable. One day a few years ago, he pulled out a whittling knife and a basswood cutout and began carving right there in his favorite coffee shop. No one threw him out, so he's been carving at the coffee house ever since.

In carving *Java John*, pictured here wearing the Scandinavian-style sweater knit for him by his favorite barista, Mocha Mary, I began by cutting the basswood blank with a band saw. Like *John*, I enjoy carving with only a single knife. But you can use whatever tools you want.

Note that *John* is looking off to one side. Carving a figure with a turned head might seem too tricky to tackle, but it's a touch that really helps bring your figure to life. You can, of course, have him looking straight ahead, but here's your chance to begin turning some heads.

Java John: Roughing Out The Carving

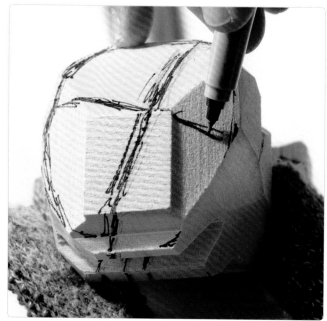

1 Sketch the major landmarks. Draw the arms. Then, draw a centerline on the rounded part of the cap. Extend the centerline from the top of the cap down into the face. This line denotes the center of the nose. Sketch a ½" (13mm)-wide nose. Draw a line perpendicular to the centerline on the top of the head, and extend the perpendicular line down both sides of the head to the shoulders. This line divides the head into the front and back. With the ears hidden by hair, the vertical line denotes the front of the hair. If ears are to be showing, place them just behind the vertical line.

2 Rough out the face. Remove wood from both sides of the nose to make the nose protrude. Refer to the pattern, and narrow and shape the face. Refer to the centerline on the top of the head to make sure the face is turned properly. Begin to round the square-shaped cap.

3 Shape the head. Narrow the head, especially in the neck and chin area. Refer to the centerline on the top of the head to make sure the sides of the head are parallel to the centerline. Because the head is turned to the right, make sure the right side of the face is carved back so it does not protrude farther than the left side of the face.

Java John shares many characteristics with the trolls, but his expression is more pleasant and his features less exaggerated.

4 **Shape the arms, back, and cap.** Carve a groove to separate the bill from the top of the cap. Round the back of the cap and the bottom of the hair. Remove wood from in front of and behind both arms. Shape the bend of the arm and the seat of the pants. The area where the legs join the trunk of the body in back reminds me of a capital letter T.

5 **Shape the front of the legs and the sweater.** Make a stop cut along the bottom of the sweater and carve up to it. Make a few large, deliberate cuts to remove the hard edges from the sweater. Carve an upside-down letter V to form the crotch of the pants where the legs join the trunk of the body.

6 **Refine the pants.** Round the top of the pockets. Shape the lumpy pockets (with the hands inside them).

7 **Shape the shoes.** Carve the wood from between the shoes. Carve the curved upper to the rounded toes. Then, shape the bottoms of the shoes so the heels are narrower than the fronts. Stop-cut around the bottoms of the pants and carve up to the stop cuts to separate the pants from the shoes.

Java John: Carving The Details

8 **Draw the mouth and smile lines.** The smile lines, or nasal-labial folds, begin at the top of the wide part of the nose (the bulb) and angle downward. Draw the mouth close to the nose, no more than 20–25% of the distance from the bottom of the nose to bottom of the chin.

9 **Carve the smile lines and mouth.** Use the tip of the knife to carve deep stop cuts slightly angled toward the mouth. Hold the knife at a lower angle and relieve up to the stop cuts to create the smile lines. Use the tip of the knife to carve the mouth groove. Round the cheeks, nose, and chin.

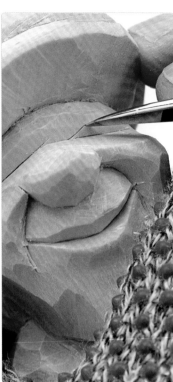

10 **Finish the sweater.** Draw the ribbed waist around the bottom front and back of the sweater. Make a stop cut on the line, and carve up to it to reduce the thickness of the waist and separate it from the rest of the sweater. Draw and carve V-grooves to represent the ribbing. Make shallow stop cuts around the top of the sweater to define the stripes at the yoke. Round the stripes slightly.

11 **Carve the eyes.** Practice first on a piece of scrap wood and then carve the project. 1) Lightly incise two triangle-shaped eyes. Then, use a delicate vertical cut to divide both triangles in half. 2) Use a chip carving-style cut to carefully remove the left half of each eye. 3) Deepen the carved triangle if desired. Remove a small triangular chip from the right corner.

FRONT   **LEFT**   **BACK**

Java John Patterns

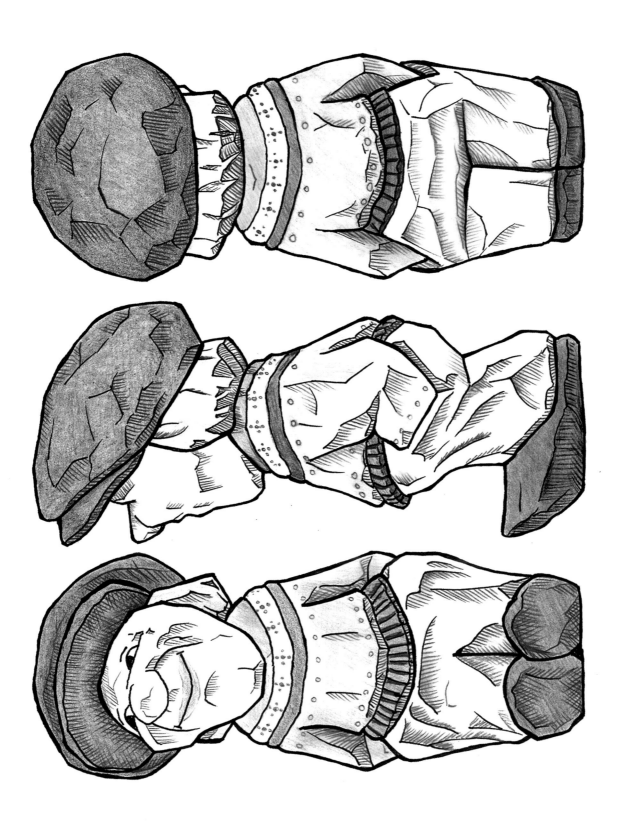

Mocha Mary

Mary has always been a hard worker, bubbling to the top in all of her many professions: student, archeologist, grocer, librarian, race-car driver, log-house restorer. But nothing provided the pleasure and satisfaction she has experienced since she opened a coffee shop a few years ago. Sure, it's hard work; she has to wake up early to get coffee going and muffins in the oven. But come 6:30 a.m., *Mary* unlocks the front door and her loyal customers begin trickling, and then pouring, in. Ah—her extended family, whom she has not seen since…yesterday. *Mocha Mary's* day has officially begun, and the coffee shop has sprung to life.

Mary is depicted here ready to serve a cup of coffee to one of her favorite customers, who earned the nickname "Java John" after he began carving right there in the coffee shop. The other customers were fascinated when he brought out his whittling knife and began working on a small basswood figure, so he's whittled coffee shop characters ever since. *Mary* or another member of her devoted army— always in uniform—even sweeps up the wood chips as he packs up to leave.

Carve this delightful coffee shop owner and customize her with glued-on accessories.

FRONT

RIGHT

BACK

LEFT

Patterns

Now, with four completed figures looking on admiringly, providing inspiration and encouragement, it's time to expand and build on what you already know.

This chapter features patterns for additional figures, together with a bit of background on some of the characters and suggestions for finishing techniques.

In order to fit all the patterns onto the page, some of them have been reduced in size from my original designs. Note that a grid has been drawn over the pattern. If you enlarge the pattern so that each square in the grid equals 1" (25mm), you'll have the pattern restored to full size. You can reduce or enlarge these patterns as much as you like.

You should also feel free, as you gain more confidence, to customize or modify these patterns. For instance, if you want *Oskar* to hold a hoe or fishing pole in his right hand, refer to the *Troll King* (p. 12) for an example of a right hand extended rather than thrust into the pocket. Or, conversely, if you prefer to exclude an element or two from one of the patterns, feel free to do that as well.

Oskar (p. 32) as a college graduate, in cap and gown? *Willie* (p. 59) with a hat? Why not?

Nisse Mor

The *Nisse Mor* (mor means mother) featured here can have a gouge-grooved skirt, described in the instructions for carving *Sara* on page 33. Note that her face is not rugged and angular but softly rounded. Her hands are tucked under her apron, which can be decorated with stripes or floral designs. Her hat could also be decorated, perhaps with a border near the bottom. The colors could be somewhat brighter than those on an immigrant figure, but earth tones would still be most appropriate.

Oskar

Oskar and *Sara* (see opposite page) were the first in their Scandinavian community to immigrate to America, leading the pack more than a century ago.

Sara

After a stormy crossing and a seemingly endless train ride, *Oskar* and *Sara* finally arrived at their new home, a recently settled community in western Minnesota. Here we see *Sara* wearing the clothes in which she arrived. Her scarf was probably brown or red iron oxide, her cape dark brown or black, and her skirt brown or dark blue. Since her clothing was undoubtedly made from rather heavy handwoven material, large, flat planes are appropriate for it. Her face can initially be carved in the same way as *Oskar's*, but then the rough, angular features should be rounded, either with a knife or a gouge, to give her a softer, more feminine look. A deeply rounded gouge, approximately ¼" [6mm] wide, can also be used to make some random vertical grooves in her skirt to create the impression of flowing material.

Johannes

Although *Oskar* and *Sara* decided to emigrate, nearby cottagers *Johannes* and *Kristina* (see page 36) were not able to take that step. Their economic plight was no better, but family commitments made the move impossible. However, after a while, their economic conditions did improve, partially because almost half of the population in their community eventually left for the United States or Canada and the pie no longer had to be divided into quite as many pieces.

Johannes is holding a homemade pitchfork, made entirely of wood. Starting with a naturally formed branch that serves as the handle and middle tine, matching tines are then whittled and pegged onto the handle, resulting in a three-tined pitchfork. His left side, with hand in pocket, is carved according to the same general instructions as for *Java John's* pocketed hands.

Johannes' Pitchfork

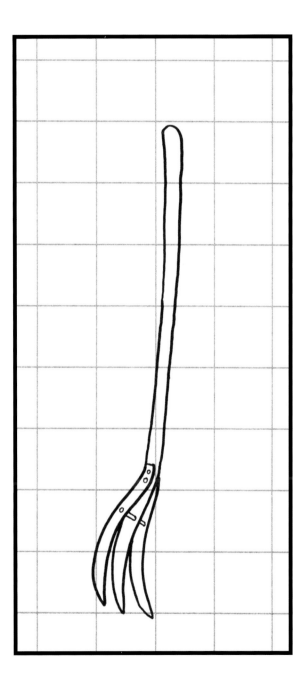

Kristina

Kristina is out raking hay. The handle of her wooden rake is inserted through the ³⁄₁₆" [5mm] hole drilled through her right hand. The rake's teeth are whittled pegs inserted into ¼" [6mm] holes in the head of the rake. *Kristina's* left arm simply hangs at her side. She could be wearing an off-white apron, a dark-green or brown skirt, a beige blouse, and a red iron oxide scarf.

Kristina's Rake

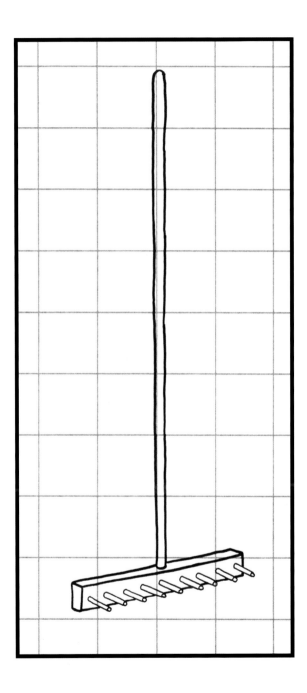

Third Generation in America

He attends the Scandinavian festivals and celebrations in the Midwest without fail. Nordic Fest, Høstfest, Lutefisk Days, Midsummer—he wouldn't miss them for the world. Although he has never been to the Old Country, he's proud to be one of its sons.

He gets carved in a similar way to the other male figures on the preceding pages. His heels should be close together, with his toes pointing out. To aid in removing wood from between his arms and body, a small hole can be drilled to get started. Color choices could include a muted blue for his bib overalls, red for his shirt, and green for his seed cap. This fellow requires a piece of wood measuring 3" by 3" by 11" [76mm by 76mm by 279mm] but, of course, can be scaled down if you prefer.

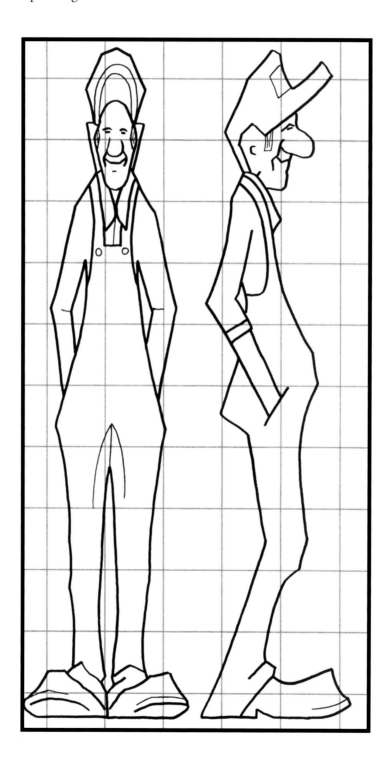

Ice Fisherman

To be able to sit out on the ice like this for hours at a time, one needs to invoke the spirit of St. Halvor the Patient, patron saint of woodcarvers and fishermen.

This fisherman and bucket can be carved as one piece, or the bucket can be sawn off and carved separately, and the figure seated on it after the carving is completed. The latter method makes it much easier to access the back and inside of his legs during the carving process.

Carve a separate piece for the fishing pole, and insert it into a ³⁄₁₆" [5mm] hole drilled into his hands as shown. Also, small holes can be drilled into opposite sides of the wide end of the bucket, into which ends of a piece of wire can be inserted, forming a handle.

After having been painted in earth tones (although he could be brightened up a bit with a red scarf) and oiled, he can be mounted on a base of your choice. Drill a tiny (no larger than ¹⁄₁₆" [2mm]) hole through the base, and string a length of elastic thread through the hole. Tie one end to the end of the fishing pole to indicate a fishing line. Draw the thread snugly through the base and knot it underneath. This will give the line a taut look, as if there were a lead sinker or bait on the end.

Woodchopper

This woodchopper is determined. No hair is visible on him since his arms touch the sides of his head, and only his cap shows from the back because it runs all the way down his collar. His hands should be left large and stylized to provide ample material for the hole (marked with dotted lines) through which the axe handle will go. After drilling a tiny pilot hole through his hands, enlarge the hole to ¼" [6mm]. Once the axe is carved, cut off about ½" [13mm] of the axe handle (the flared end) and insert it into the hole from the top of the carving. The axe should be inserted so that the head is down and near his back. This position guarantees a powerful swing. One way you can create buttons on this figure is to drill holes (no larger than ³⁄₁₆" [5mm]) and insert round, whittled pegs.

Logger

The timber stands of the upper Midwest, Pacific Northwest, and Canada provided employment for countless Scandinavian immigrants, such as *Karl*. Here, he's holding a cant hook, which can be carved separately and inserted through a 5⁄16" [8mm] hole drilled through his hands as shown. The wooden cant hook handle can be either left unpainted or painted a dark yellow ochre. The metal fittings on the cant hook can be steel blue or gray. *Karl* could be wearing a black cap, red shirt, brown trousers, off-white or gray socks, and dark brown boots.

Bringing in the Firewood

Walter, here, has no time to stop for anything. He's got to bring in the wood—one of the most important chores of the day.

Carve the figure without his cargo. This allows access while carving his face (which is visible from the side even after the firewood is added) as well as his chest, the top of his arms, and the inside of his mittens.

After painting the figure in colors of your choice, add the pieces of firewood, which are carved individually and glued together in his arms.

Reading

Even though her days were filled with hard work, Eva savored those moments when she could sit down with a book. One of her brothers worked on a ship, and through her reading she got to travel with him, sailing to exotic ports of call brimming with sunshine and fresh fruit.

The log bench is carved separately. Drill four ¼" [6mm] holes into the log seat, as indicated, and insert the whittled legs.

Paint her clothing in muted earth tones of your choice.

Nisse

As with his Swedish cousin, the tomte, this Norwegian *Nisse* is the bearer of Christmas gifts in his country. Dressed quite regally here, he looks almost like Father Christmas, with his red coat and hat trimmed with white. His beard and hair are also white, but different texturing on the hair will distinguish it from the trim. (Use a V-tool on the hair and a small rounded gouge to texture the trim.) His clogs can be painted yellow ochre, darkened slightly with brown.

The Schoolteacher

Miss Barrows began teaching in a one-room country school when she was seventeen, and she continued teaching in various schools for the next hundred years. At least, that's what it seemed like to her pupils. She could be tough, but her severity was tempered by those occasions when she would hold the entire second grade (both of us) on her lap during reading. She usually wore a black or dark brown skirt and an off-white blouse.

Down a Quart

This is Sparky, a gas station attendant of an earlier era. He was there to fill the tank, check the oil and tires, clean your windshield, and fill you in on everything from driving conditions and weather reports to sports scores.

His pants can be painted either blue or olive green. His shirt and cap, perhaps featuring the logo of your favorite service station, can be painted white or "company colors."

The Gardener

When May rolls around, Gus gets his hoe out of the tool shed and begins to commune with nature, carefully tending those plants and seedlings he's been thinking about since February.

Drill a ³⁄₁₆" [5mm] hole through his hand and insert the hoe, which is carved separately. The blade of the hoe can also be carved separately and then glued onto the handle.

Outfit him in subdued colors of your choice. You may want to paint the metal portion of the hoe a bright color, such as blue, green, or red.

Alleluia

Rev. Carlson has a rather firm grip on his emotions. You'll probably never see him doubled over with laughter or shouting loudly and inappropriately. But what is more important is that he's there through thick and thin—celebrating, grieving, tending his flock.

His clerical shirt is black with a white collar. Using either glue or wood screws, mount the bust on a wooden base of your choice.

The Bird Watcher

Just as some dog owners eventually begin to resemble their pets, the beak on this bird watcher is becoming more pronounced with each passing migration.

A khaki-colored uniform would be appropriate. The pith helmet and socks are off-white, the shoes are brown, and the binoculars are black.

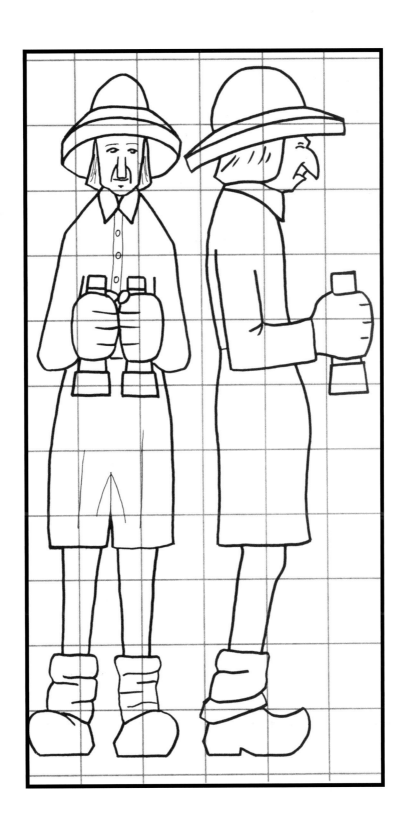

The Auditor

"I'm here to take a look at your books." Dressed in a black or dark blue suit, this *Auditor* presents a severe image.

His briefcase, sawn from ½" [13mm]-thick stock, can be carved separately. Drill a ³⁄₁₆" [5mm] hole through his hand to accommodate the handle, which can be made from either two pieces of wood, carved and glued into place, or from a piece of leather shoelace. If you prefer the leather handle, drill two ⅛" [3mm] holes into the top of the briefcase; then, thread a leather shoelace, cut to the appropriate length, through his hand and glue both ends into the holes in the briefcase.

Ed

Ed lives in a river town and has worked on riverboats nearly all his life. Note that his head is turned slightly to one side. He's watching a neophyte pilot trying to dock. The smirk on his face suggests that HE could do it better, and he enjoys watching the young whippersnapper sweat. *Ed* usually dresses all in black. If you prefer to see *Ed* wearing a different kind of cap, simply leave more wood on the top to accommodate different headgear.

Herbertine

Back in the Old Country, before they immigrated to North America, her parents wanted a son; they already had four daughters. They had even chosen a name for their son-to-be: Herbert. But then came daughter #5… so they named her *Herbertine* (her-burr-TEEN-uh).

Her friends and family agree that her personality is as unique and wonderful as her name. Drill a hole through her right hand, as indicated, to accommodate her parasol.

Olaf

Olaf is another version of a nisse or tomte, the friendly little guy who serves as the bringer of gifts at holiday time in Scandinavia. *Olaf* typically wears a red cap with white trim, a yellow ochre (or blue or green) jacket, dark blue knickers, red socks, and wood-colored clogs.

Tomte with Stick

The tomte (Swedish), or nisse (Norwegian), is the bearer of Christmas gifts in Scandinavia. But he and his colleagues are around during other parts of the year as well. Back during the time when most people lived on farms, the tomte usually lived in the barn. If treated well, he could be counted on to help around the farm—but if mistreated or scoffed at, the tomte could also be mischievous.

This *Tomte* has a walking stick in his right hand, not quite as tall as he is, whittled separately and inserted through the hole indicated in the pattern. The hole is ¼" [6mm] in diameter, but drill a pilot hole first.

When drilling the hole, align it so that the walking stick doesn't jab into the top of his foot but touches the ground just beside it. He also has a homemade backpack woven from birch bark. Using a V-tool or a knife tip, carve lines to indicate a basket-weave pattern.

His beard could be white, his cap red (with a red or white ball), his jacket green or red, and his mittens and backpack a golden color. (The white side of the birch-bark strips should face inward.) His shoes could be yellow ochre, brown, or brownish-green, depending on where and how long he has worn them.

Tante Trine

Tante Trine (TAHN-tuh TREEN-uh), or "Aunt Trine," comes to visit about once a year. She's a little old-fashioned, especially in the way she dresses (dark brown skirt, dark green coat, black hat with red trim), but the kids can hardly wait for her visits. They love her bedtime stories, as well as the box of fresh, homemade doughnuts she always brings along.

Golfer

He may never make it to St. Andrews, but he tries to dress the part nonetheless. His sweater vest, shirt, and argyle socks are all in pastel colors. You can make his golf shoes into saddle shoes, if you prefer. And finally, refer to a real golf club or putter as a model for the one you'll carve and insert through the ³⁄₁₆" [5mm] hole drilled through his right hand.

Chore Time

When Selma went out to help with evening chores (feeding the calves; milking cows, including sharing a little fresh, warm milk with the four or five barn cats; and closing the door of the chicken house for the night), this is how she dressed: blue jeans, dark green jacket, and a red bandana-like kerchief.

Captain

Dressed in his dark blue uniform, brass (yellow ochre) buttons, white shirt, and white or black cap (with black brim), the *Captain* always cut a striking image. Carve an appropriately sized pipe if you'd like, which can be inserted into a ⅛" [3mm] hole drilled at the very end of his mouth.

Willie

Willie was never much of an athlete, but he could run circles around other craftsmen in town when it came to the masterpieces that emerged from his woodworking shop. His ancestors, all of whom emigrated from Sweden, would have been proud if they could have seen his woodcarving, his scroll-saw creations, and his lathe work. If you think *Willie* should have a bit more hair or a hat, leave some extra wood on his head and make him as hairy as you'd like.

Richard

Richard LOVES to chop wood. And he's good at it, too. One whack and that piece of oak flies apart. Ah…more firewood for the months to come. He typically wears a red wool shirt, a black cap (with optional yarn ball on top carved separately and inserted), and blue or green trousers…plus brown lumberjack boots. For a model of a hatchet or an axe, whichever you prefer, refer to p. 40.

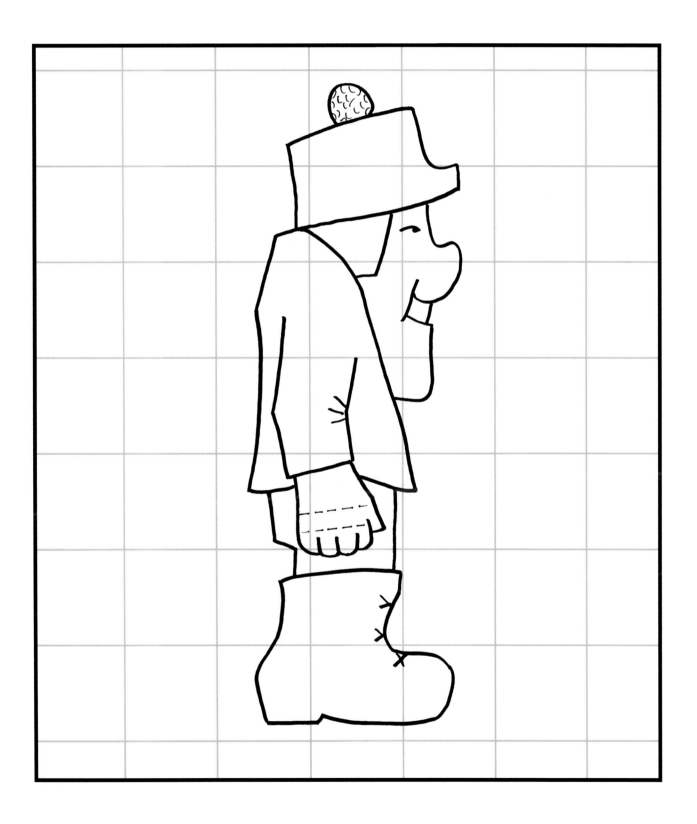

Leprechaun

Thanks to trips to Ireland by Vikings a thousand years ago, nearly every nisse in Norway or tomte in Sweden has a third or fourth cousin in Ireland: who else—a *Leprechaun*. Painted in bright Irish green with black shoes (ochre buckles), white socks, and a carrot-colored beard, he has a walking stick inserted into the ³⁄₁₆" [5mm] hole drilled through his right hand.

Baker

Gladys found steady employment as a "hired girl," helping busy farm wives with cleaning, washing, and baking. Dressed in wooden clogs, red kerchief, dark green skirt, white blouse, and off-white apron, her hands support a serving tray or breadboard (carved separately and glued on after the figure is painted). Carve an appropriately sized pie, loaf of bread, cake, etc. to place on the tray. The baked goods she's holding could reflect your own favorite family recipes or ethnic/holiday food.

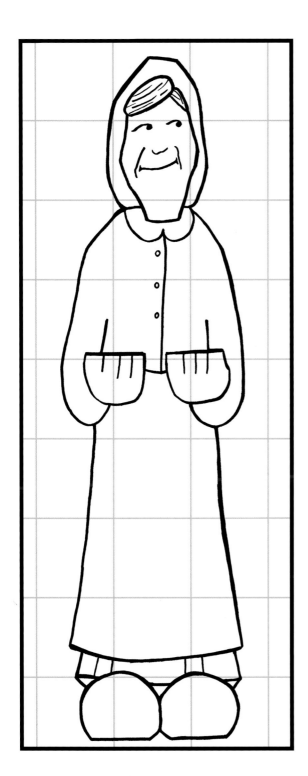
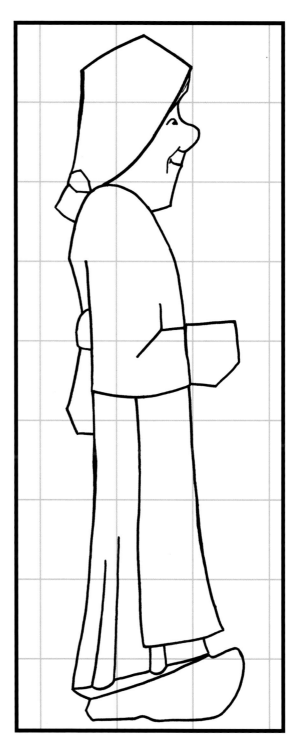

Online

Erik likes to work at home, even though he doesn't have a very elaborate home office. Carve his body and the seat of the stool on which he's sitting together, all in one piece; then drill ¼" [6mm] holes into the underside of the stool and insert three or four pegs. Carve pieces for the taller chair and assemble the chair. Carve an appropriately sized computer for Erik to use—what home office would be complete without one?

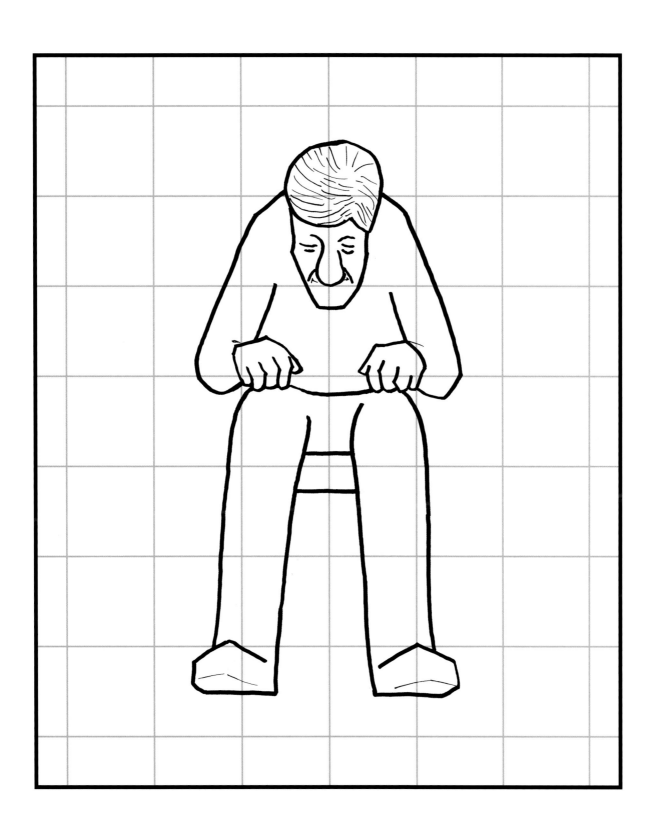

Hansen

Despite his sometimes-unruly pupils, *Hansen* loved his job as a teacher. Book (carved connected to his body...not carved separately and inserted) tucked under his arm, clad in conservative black, he looks confident and ready to begin his day of teaching. Sixteen pupils, grades 1-8, await his arrival in the small one-room country school. It might sound quite rural and parochial, but *Hansen* opened their eyes and minds to a vast and exciting world: Marco Polo...sailing ships... migrating butterflies...pirates...mathematics...

The Whittler

There is plenty of room on the handle of this laminated Swedish Mora knife, sometimes also referred to as a Swedish carving knife or a sloyd knife, to carve something interesting. And if one intends to use the knife for carving or whittling, what better subject could there be than a whittler!

Transfer the shape of the handle onto a practice piece, such as a scrap of soft basswood or pine. Carve a prototype to make sure that despite its carved surface, the handle still fits comfortably in your hand. Also, if a different style of knife handle is being carved, facial features and proportions may have to be altered slightly from the pattern presented here.

Caution: Be sure to make a blade guard before beginning to carve a handle. (A double thickness of cardboard taped securely around the blade should do nicely.)

Once carved, the handle can be painted and/or oiled.

Letter Opener

Saw the letter opener from ¼" [6mm] or ³⁄₁₆" [5mm] material. Carve the head as shown, using a V-tool for detail in the beard, hat, and hair. In shaping the blade, imagine a two-edged knife blade. The center remains thicker, but it thins down to form cutting edges on both sides. Paint the cap red and the trim and beard white. The blade can either be painted or left a natural wood color.

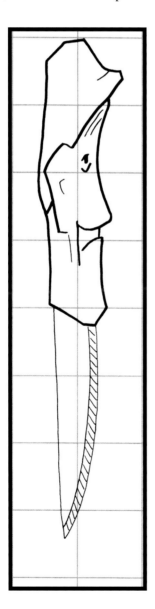

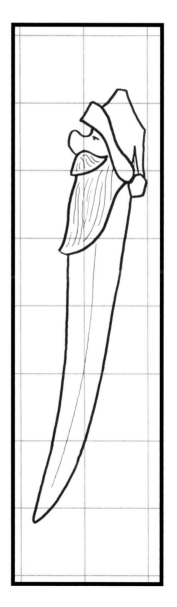

Politician

Senator Long has served for many terms. He runs on his name: Long on honesty...Long on optimism... Long on hard work, on behalf of the people of his state. He wears a navy blue suit, white shirt, red tie, and black shoes. (If he takes off his jacket, you can see that he also sports red suspenders, a white belt, and a very fat wallet.)

Ale Hen Candle Holder

The design for this candle holder is based on a traditional Scandinavian ale hen, or Ladel. Bandsaw the piece from 1⅛" [29mm]-thick or 1¼" [32mm]-thick basswood or pine. Sand the entire piece, and then V-tool in the design as shown. Drill a ¾" [19mm] vertical hole (or appropriately larger, if you will be using brass candle holder inserts, available from woodcraft suppliers) for the candle. The piece can be left natural (finished with satin varnish or oil) or can be painted in colors of your choice.

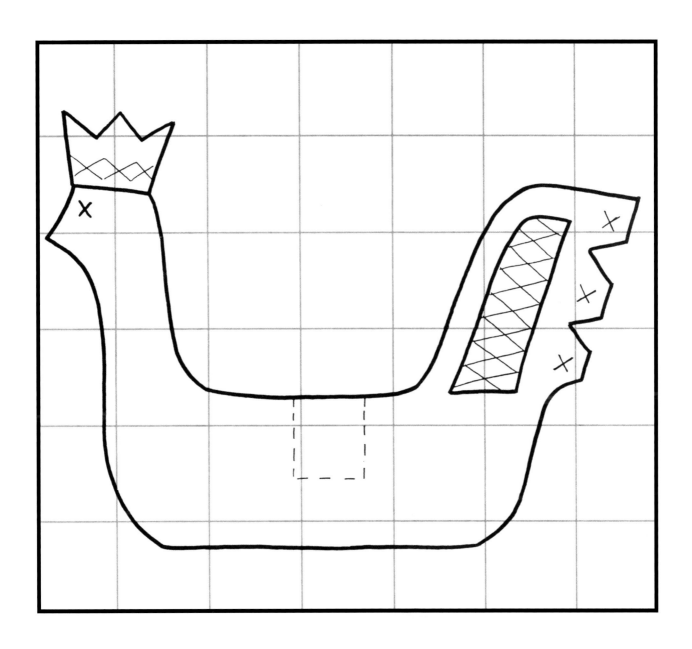

Rooster 1

Inspired by traditional Swedish roosters, this modernized version can be decorated in a variety of ways. If left unpainted, it could be decorated with woodburning or chip carving. If painted, feel free to refer to design books, photos of painted eggs, etc.

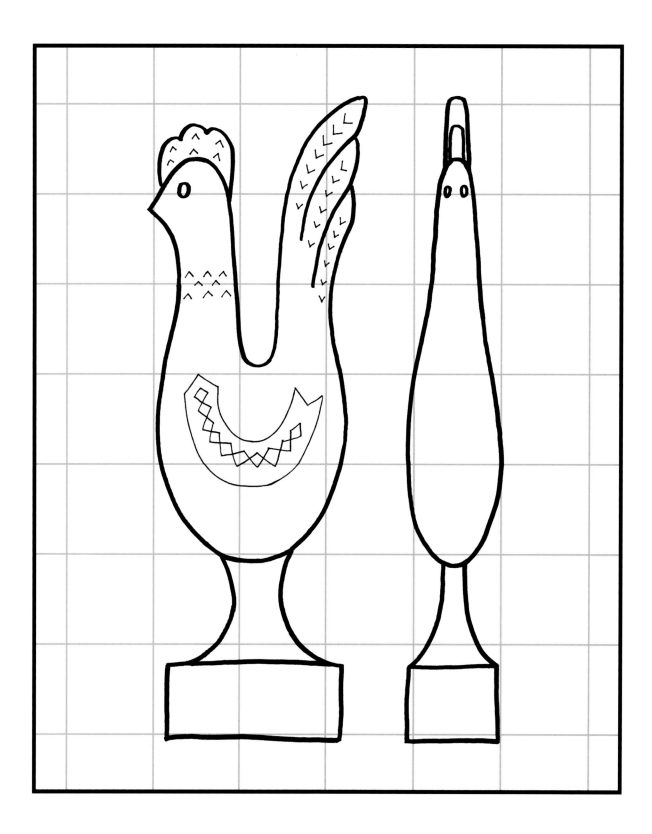

Rooster 2

Here's another version featuring slightly angular lines.

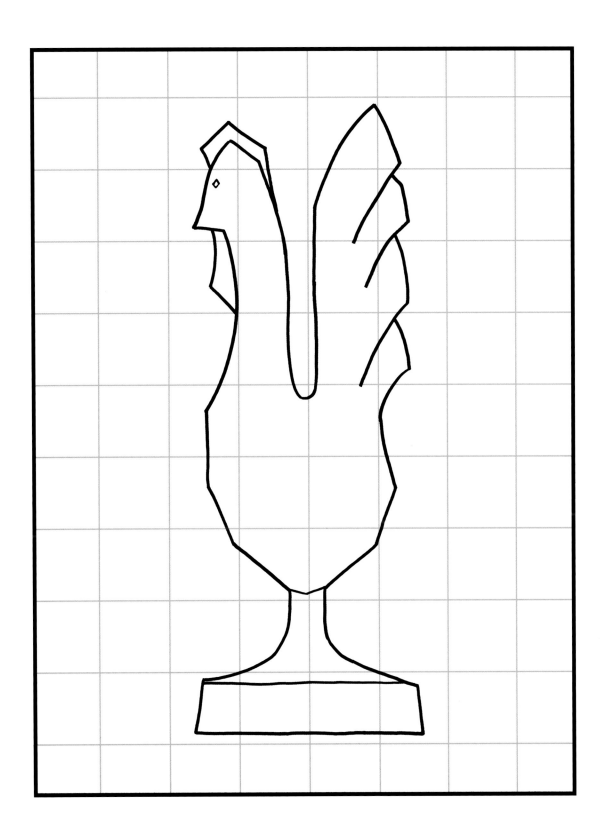

Horse 1

Here are several patterns for a tradtional Dalecarlian horses. They are usually painted bright colors, like red, blue, and green, and decorated with small paintable flowers.

Horse 2

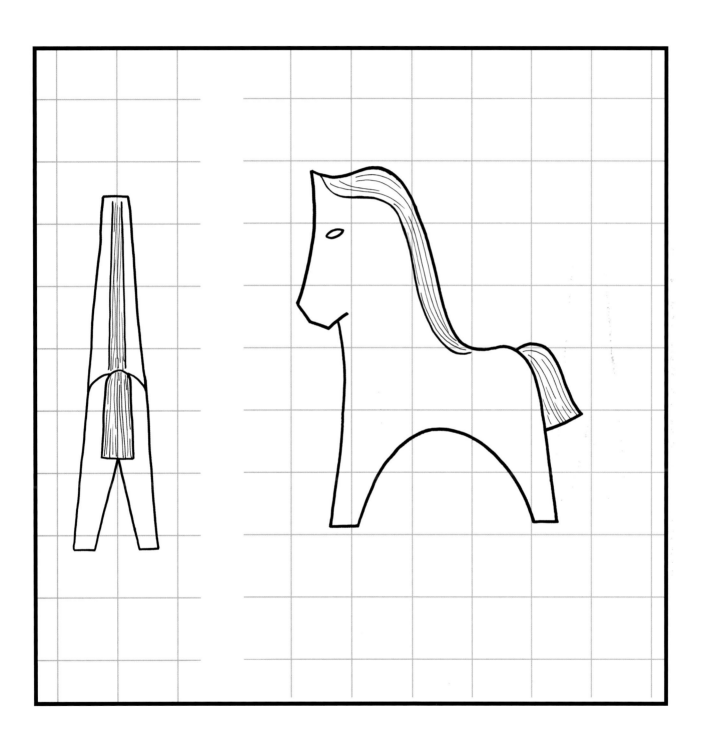

Horse 3

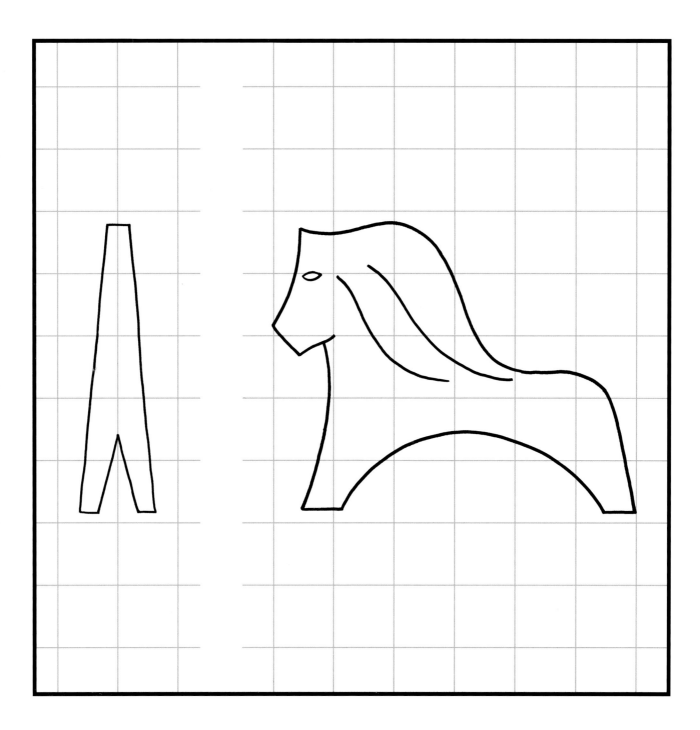

Horse 4

Ornaments

Saw these holiday ornaments from ¼" [6mm] material. Drill a ¹⁄₁₆" [2mm] hole through each ornament; the dot on the patterns indicates hole placement. Later, thread a cord through the hole to hang the ornaments on a tree.

Surface-carve the front side with a V-tool. Sand the back. (Or, if you prefer, you can carve both sides.) Carve off the sharp corners so that the ornament resembles a cookie.

Paint the ornaments with appropriate holiday colors. Since I want my Christmas ornaments to help create a bright, festive atmosphere, I don't thin the acrylic paint with as much water as when I'm painting muted turn-of-the-century immigrant figures.

Finally, wooden stands can be made so that the ornaments can be placed on a shelf or table instead of hung on a tree. Rip a ¾" [19mm]-wide by ¼" [6mm] deep groove the entire length of the strip. Saw the strip into pieces approximately 2" [50mm] long. Sand the pieces on all surfaces, and they will make ideal stands for your ornaments.

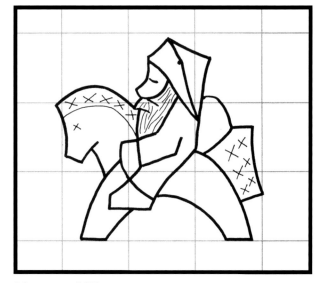

Mounted Nisse

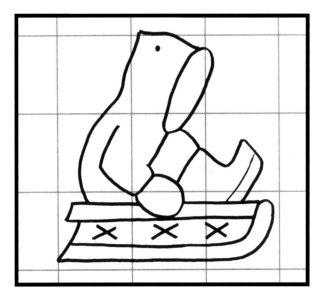

Sledder

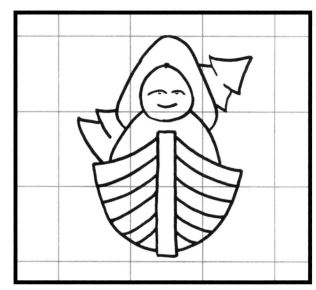

Home for the Holidays

Tomte, or Nisse

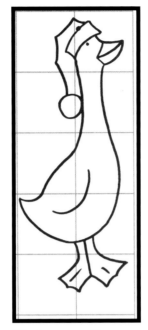

Christmas Goose

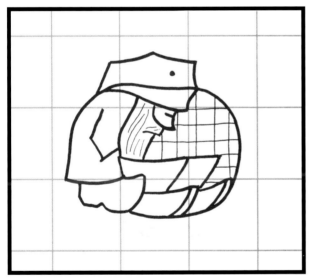

Christmas Morning

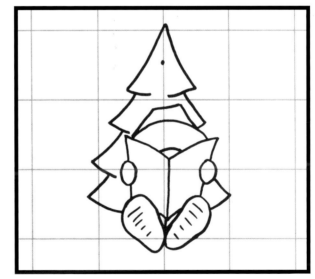

The Christmas Story

Holiday Candle Holder

Saw this piece to shape from ⅜" [10mm]-thick stock. Drill a vertical hole to accommodate a birthday candle as indicated. (Based on the size of the candle you will be using, the hole should be approximately ³⁄₁₆" [5mm].) Surface-carve the entire figure, and then V-tool his features as shown. His beard, as well as the base, can be painted white. His robe is red, and his cap and mittens can be either red or bright green.

Index

Note: Page numbers in *italics* indicate patterns/projects.